Introduction to an American Humorist
I Believe

by

Susan Barbara Shapiro: SBS

DORRANCE PUBLISHING CO., INC.
PITTSBURGH, PENNSYLVANIA 15222

The contents of this work including, but not limited to, the accuracy of events, people, and places depicted; opinions expressed; permission to use previously published materials included; and any advice given or actions advocated are solely the responsibility of the author, who assumes all liability for said work and indemnifies the publisher against any claims stemming from publication of the work.

Dorrance Publishing Co., Inc.
701 Smithfield Street
Pittsburgh, PA 15222
Visit our website at *www.dorrancebookstore.com*

ISBN: 978-1-4349-1267-1
eISBN: 978-1-4349-3981-4

To Nigel, my talking cat

I have never loved so wisely
or
so well
Mommy
SBS

At age four
I heard I said:

I'm going to be a hero when I grow up.
            ?

I would like
the cloth cover

to be
green.

The color of
life
and
me.

I would like to syndicate

these books

nationally in newspapers

on

Thursday

queer day.

As presented by Dorrance Publishing Co., Inc.

Man could not believe in his own perfection.
He reached beyond himself to see if there was a being who is greater.
God was created to prove man's premise:
He is imperfect.
    So it begins…

I Believe

Susan Barbara Shapiro
The Humorist

I chronicle

using

quotables.

Quotables

Dedicated to

Nigel
The Talking Cat.

I have never loved so wisely or so well.

Mommy

People r
        u
           l
              e

If your neighbor has more than you, you have the better view.

* * * * * *

It's awful to believe every day isn't a brand new day, and that anything can happen as a child.

* * * * * *

Don't systematize yourselves. No one should suffer for trying your welcome.

* * * * * *

Wouldn't it be nice to know that we can't go below unfathomable, water seeks its own level.

* * * * * *

Don't allow too much of your lives to be routine and boring. I've done it, you can, too.

* * * * * *

You got your one vote Hitler; Adolph God's.

* * * * * *

Someone was nice to you. You be nice to someone else.

* * * * * *

People who are big shots are usually unknown.

* * * * * *

It used to be that one's immortality lies in one's child(ren). Now, 2010, immortality is achievable in oneself.

* * * * * *

Please note, I have no rights over God.

* * * * * *

Anthropologist for the biological state of Nigel.

* * * * * *

Christ died, but he left behind "You."

* * * * * *

resumé including proof of my possessing both language and sciences. Art and science fused as one in fact.

* * * * * *

In mind, I have Samuel Clemens as my lawyer now. Mark Twain is his pen name.

* * * * * *

Grateful with pleasured hands. Pleasure. Thank you.

* * * * * *

Neuroleptics series

lithium

Navane
Melleril
Prolixin
Stellizine   been there
Clozapine   done that
Therazine
Risperdone: non-neuroleptic
too long-frazzled brain

* * * * * *

Clinton coming, I'm last great thinker; only one to achieve normalcy.
gone   green

```
            a                t    e
        p       SBS      o       v
        p     green      g    e
          r              e    r
            o            t    y
          v              h    o
            e     e    n
            d   r    e
```

Who?

everyone represented

You don't fight the fight, youngster. You live the life.
    Susan
v   SBS
    Miss Shapiro
Lester: She's one way. Chauncy Street.

Susan: I've never been there.

Star Trek

Gene Roddenberry's
A Favorite Episode

At the end of war between the federation and a lizard race, Kirk says as he pins the captain down and stops: I can't kill you. You are the most repelling, repulsive form of life our race has ever hated or feared. But you thought you were trying to protect your people as any captain would. I'll spare your life.

Up pops the most advanced gentle lives ever to be or have ever been and says:

By your act, Captain Kirk, we feel in 1,000 years you'll have hope and be hope to us.

Congratulations!

An episode

Joke

The Cat's on the Roof

Stanley calls his brother, "Hi, Dave. How's my cat."

"He's dead."

Stanley, the brother calling, says: "Why did you just blurt that out? Why didn't you tell me slow? Why didn't you say, the cat's on the roof. And then tell me he broke his leg and you had to take him to the hospital. Then tell me he got an infection and that they did everything they could for him but the infection spread too far and he passed away."

"Well, anyway, how's Mom?"

"Mom's on the roof."

The Evolution of Expression

by
Charles Wesley Emerson

Begun, 1880
Emerson College
Boston, Massachusetts
(Beacon Street)
You may remember: Rod Serling
"You are now entering the twilight zone."

* * * * * *

One woman's fight with the concept called mental illness
Sound-meaning-truth. Separated by actuality, positive green-yellow negative.
I haven't gotten to Esther yet, but let me preface: she isn't nature's treasure.
Dead Esther was my "mother." Yet, Huntington Hospital—year 1990 something, sorry—took blood and wrote me after genetically testing: I was 'genetically pure.'"
To continue…

* * * * * *

If you look better in Hell than Lucifer, he's in Hell not you.

* * * * * *

You don't get what you want from someone else.

* * * * * *

My two beautiful 'black' bosses: Robert Jordan and Tenyka Sheriff are going to take on Esther (dead Esther). Derek Miller (the United Nations representative of black people as knowledge), Alan Shapiro (a judge pro tiem), the Supreme Court of the land and everybody.

All for

Miss Shapiro   Truth only?

Humor lost?

And win.

* * * * * *

Most immigrants pass through immigration and pass. Instead of being thrown back where they came from.

Why don't we get the rich, famous, gorgeous ones? Have you ever been or seen an immigrant?

Meet Esther's "immigrant Annie," Barney's wife, Esther's brother. Five brothers, two girls: Sally, eleven years older than pooped out Esther, "the baby."

When I came along, the first girl in the family (where they got me from I don't know yet), there's ten days missing from my birth and when the doctor said I was born. And at eight years old, Esther tells me of my birth as "girl": "You'd think little Jesus Christ was born."

So begins the "mental illness" approach to Esther and Lester Shapiro.

* * * * * *

Noah's ark through black Bill Cosby's comedy album isn't out till I'm a teen. And many years later, the illness called "Are you hearing voices?" begins.

Lucky me.

* * * * * *

I learned my sense of humor from adversity. In my early years, it was my parents who held on to me to secure their freedom by taking mine.

That's probably why I come through with humor in the face of all and any adversity.

* * * * * *

Sylvia:
A person so lacking in ability, she needs to kill those who are to be what she is. Also, my mother's or rather just Esther's niece, Barney and immigrant Annie's child, second born. The first one is a real ditz.

* * * * * *

Man met dog.
Dog allowed man to touch him.
Man's knowledge of self-hate begins.
Made up argument,
                Dog, backward is God.

* * * * * *

Wherever children are, life will be.

* * * * * *

Eight hundred dollars a month on social security buys you your locks on your doors.
—New York
Wait till I explain: New York suck up.

* * * * * *

My doors are never locked against my neighbor.

* * * * * *

After World War II (WWII), all military men from all coasts came to the European theatre led by General Eisenhower. And as they

walked, the smell of death was up in their noses that they knew they were coming to another death camp sixty miles away.

At that point, Eisenhower began the Vietnam War to trail us for decades to come.

* * * * * *

If you're a good person, good things will happen to you.

* * * * * *

Germany   Ike
apple
pie

n
o
i   ?
c
e
d

South Vietnam

p
i   ?
s
s
i
m   Mexico
y
t
h
g
i
m

Gulf of Mexico route, possible.

* * * * * *

I've been seriously hurt, being on supplemental security income. They named it "disability."

* * * * * *

Still needed: regulatory behavior.

* * * * * *

                                        Prolixin, taking
                                        Cogentin
                                              Neuroleptics
                                                  outdated
                                        Restoril
                                ten pills at night
                                thirty years ago
                                              Space: legal (hold?)
                                                  Now, again,
                                                      thirty years later,
                                back.

  I
    h
      e
        a
         r
you.
                    Mark Twain
                    Chronicler

                          (hold)

* * * * * *

Substitute instructional assistant employing behavioral modification techniques: Lift, diaper, feed special handicapped children in least restrictive environment—school setting.

* * * * * *

Samuel, you looked at another humorist when introduced (the rope man, Will Rodgers), and found yourself lacking

                                        Mark Twain
                                        "mine for now"

* * * * * *

An expression of mine
You're not that high on the evolutionary scale.
Before, I studied
evolution with a language chapter.

* * * * * *

For you to know. Cry
    cry
        baby   Nigel coming
   cry
    cry
        baby   Janis Joplin: Queen
                      of '70s rock.

* * * * * *

Good-bye Joel
   Silver bells and golden needles
   will not mend this heart of mine.
   And I will not be warmed in the coolness of your wine.
First husband.
Hello, Richard, after decent interval of time.
I married twice. I had two boys.
Derek Brad Miller, 1970
Andrew Justin Sheehan, 1976
   Alone since 1979, California-bound after divorce from my love, Richard, my true love. Never went with anyone seriously or even friendship of a personal nature since 1982. Andy came to live in the Los Angeles area like me. Derek settled in Europe.
   My life was basically the sweetness of life. Work, school, California State University, Los Angeles, seven years. Work of a physical nature, thirteen years. Writing complete, length of time, and here we are.

Immigrants
You come from all over the world.
When you register to vote, you are called to jury duty...
               as an American.
      All seated,
               the honorable judge is in session.
It's up to you now new Americans.

* * * * * *

How do you keep them down on the farm after they've seen Paris? If then, if then, if then, Chicken Little.

* * * * * *

Stop.
Red light district.

* * * * * *

The first step in hearing voices is to be what I am regularly, a teacher: stand up and say your name.

* * * * * *

Here comes stupid Esther and stupid Lester. Here comes the Noah's ark routine by Bill Cosby (black).
"Noah."
Noah looks around but doesn't see anyone.
"Noah."
Here's the mistake. Noah answers, "Yes?"
"It's the Lord, Noah."
Noah responds (mine not Cosby's). I've heard about you in Temple (University? Where Cosby got his PhD?)
"I want you to make an ark."
He did. All the animals (in twos) were saved with his family. And the family of man began again, with a covenant of a rainbow never to flood man again.

* * * * * *

Back to God again.
God so loved the world that he gave his only begotten Son that whoever shall believe in Him shall have eternal life.
Enjoy
SBS

The story of God
by
SBS

Man met God.
Man was bored by God.
God made woman.
Man was happy.
Until woman opened her mouth against God.
God found out.
Man took the blame.
And then:
And then?
And then?

And so the world became until God Junior was born. God got back with man and sent his son into the world 'cause God loved the lousy world so much that the story of God continued. Man got even with God by nailing his son to a cross.
Cross blades came.
Lousy ending for a lousy world and story.

* * * * * *

This chronicler is like a newspaper, which is why I've tried placement in newspapers across our great Nation on queer day for you to have fun.
To keep you eternally,
The Lord

Nigel: "You may be the Lord, but I'm the cat."
So begins my worship of the cat in America, with love to Russia and Egypt, especially.

* * * * * *

"Susan" means princess of the Nile. I've had my feet shackled in a mental hospital (stupid dead Esther and dead Lester, obviously not at that time, but still) where I regressed back to being an eight-year-old in my fury and existed as a Russian princess. They had to feed me. And then righteousness took hold and I was, quite quickly, released. So much for Esther and Lester Shapiro (deceased).

* * * * * *

This was an aside note: the newspapers say it easy for you but keep you informed; the general public, to act as you will.

How you get there is everything.

* * * * * *

An expression of mine that I've taken beyond death: two being one—me, Susan, and Susan, my creation, which turned out to be my truth. I hope you'll get a chance to see her come in. It's breathtaking.

* * * * * *

You're only as fast as your littlest one.

I always go no faster than the littlest one and I haven't met him/her yet.

* * * * * *

God was personal with his people.

z

* * * * * *

The Southern man worked himself into a dependency on the black.

* * * * * *

For Christ's sake I sing, "I believe in miracles." (God singing to Mother Mary, "since you came along...you sexy thing, you sexy thing...")

Here's where Robert the monk comes in, with his 5,000 men (ouch).

> "I never really believed in Jesus,
> but I sometimes still pray to Mary.
> (For you who don't know)"

Mother Mary is Jesus' mother. Nice mother. She kept him un-known until he was thirty. And he began his ministry as a servant to you—he too—for your sake.

How we doin' so far?

Everybody sing!

* * * * * *

Vichey

Derek thinks he can exist as a Jew anywhere he wants, even in Vichey.

He tells us that the French resistance wasn't as great as people say it was.

* * * * * *

This Planet

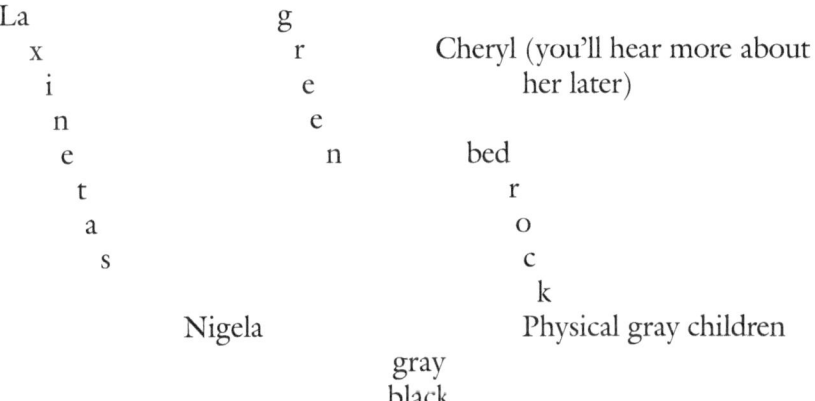

The gray (ammalgam, amalgam, Cheryl the dentist) children, re-membering the wonder of life as they close their eyes at the solid Cheryl is putting in their bodies. Death.

The black child couldn't get a hold in my palate's nonadhesive and went into ingestion.

Both to rise to glory. Mommy didn't make it. Or did I? The verdict isn't in, figuratively.

The tax board is the people.

Hooligan. Cheryl.
Every person is allowed to be at their qualifiable.

* * * * * *

Law—jobs

Gratis, $500.00, lifetime achievement award.

1. Harvard for "the word."
   Enlightened children (secondary colors and configurations) Cambridge, Massachusetts, the use of the word.
2. Calilfornia State University
   Communicative disorders. Thirty-five years recognition. Retirement, chairperson of the department.
3. Emerson College, Boston, Massachusetts.
   Communicative disorder department, chairperson CCC. Suzanne Swope Robbins, Speech and Hearing Clinic, Ohio State, bachelor and master, when master level was incredibly difficult to acquire. Money to retire—?

I have seen and been told that I have the left hand of Thomas Jefferson. By whom else but me—?

Thank you,
Sir

* * * * * *

In 1978, Richard and I were separating. This called for some action on my part. I had to go over my assets and liabilities.

I took myself to Brown University, Rhode Island for three days, where residents— including me -were allowed to use their library.

I asked the reference librarian what books she has on neuroscience. She handed me one leather bound large book.

I believe that when you go somewhere for information, you get through it to get to it.

I looked at only the speech hearing and language parts of neuroscience. I used index cards to copy the propositions.

I put together: the psycholinguistic application of oratory and rhetoric (as known to Emerson's students who keep up as I did) and establishing "communications observatory," watching out for man and God.

I completed my work in 2005-2006. Sending the creation through processes, structures, patterns, and life (green) back to the government's linguistic studies department, which began so many years ago with Dr. Paul Chapin, chairperson of the government's linguistic department.

I came to California and got established and ended my tour of California duty in The Green Hotel and Apartments, Old Town, Pasadena.

I began writing again after seven years at California State University, Los Angeles, and here I am with, hopefully, you.

Firm Belief

Any life born is a life worth keeping, to have and to hold.

I heard small children being told in courts: "I'm too little to live. I've told everyone including clergy."

No response.

I responded.

If you work real hard, the fruits of your labor will come at least at the end of your life...

We're going for socialized medicine with carrier's medical

Today, 2010, bankers are doctors and doctors are bankers. The welfare dime is solid with a psycho-social hold.

The media asked South Pasadena kids as representative of their peer groups all across the southland. Why didn't they have history?

I replied by becoming an American and world history teacher, uncredentialed, to South Pasadena and across the southland within the sound of my voice.

I call them "new age." I had them take the CBEST at the same time as their teacher. Who came out ahead?

I teach through speech, language, and hearing at a master's level without the CCC. I'm not a therapist, only a teacher and with your grace, an author/writer.

My Credo

My belief from childhood and on into my marriage with Richard: I used to wait till he went to sleep. I felt that I was too old but I couldn't fall asleep without the prayer. Here goes:
Now I lay me down to sleep
I pray the Lord my soul to take
If I should die before I wake
I pray the Lord my soul to keep.
Dear God,
Please bless my parents. Let them live a long and healthy and happy life together.
Please bless all the good people in the world and help those that are bad.
Please bless all the good animals in the world and help those that are bad.
Thank you for everything.
Please bless yourself God above all
Because without you, we're nothing.

Now, today and for the last thirty years that I know, mentioning God puts you in a mental hospital. I didn't go very often (mental hospital). Only when my "parents" sleepover and I'm reacting to God knows what. Because it's certainly nothing I know about.

I'm a pragmatist: Interaction with Susan

My prayer position:

I'd like to see Oprah turn the color purple.

The "fuck" woman—Whoopie Goldberg. The minute the camera's off, here comes Whoopie: fuck /'0*%$#.

She's obnoxious in real life. (I did some acting—*True Lies, Startrek: the Next Generation, Burke's Law*, and some more.)

They talked about Christ coming, but not through his body.

I heard him say: "You should hear (to his mother) what I hear the chosen people (Jews) want to do to me when I grow up."

The prophecy of his legacy.

* * * * * *

Christ

I've only been granted the color green; the color of life. My birthright didn't hold the one in Boston, Massachusetts. But my heritage holds me.

"He bows his head to Jesus, goes for Uncle Sam (my hatred of Lester and Esther's having a child of carnage and blood slaughter: Alan Phillip Shapiro) during the war.

He only loved one woman was the spirit of this small town Southern man.

I saved Neil Young's "Southern Man" all my adult life through Richard, my beloved husband. Andy, I've prepared for "Why did you marry my father?" And I could tell him and through living vision (one of my creations for your sake and mine) Roberta Flack's "The First Time Ever I Saw Your Face."

Boston Garden's Emerson College 1970-71 me 1967-69 Graduation. Richard, Joseph Sheehan, and I, Susan Barbara Shapiro, met down Cape Cod. My parents had a cape house—four bedrooms, two in the loft for me and Derek. He was two and a half when we started going.

My girlfriend, Janie Sharon, had a ranch house with her parents down the cape, one mile away. They were working people, including Janie.

My parents' house was next to a cemetery and the front of the house had no entrance because of the incredible pine trees in front. The door was there, opening into a living room that they never used. They sat in the breezeway next to the back door.

Next to the house was a structure they used to display their antiques, mostly marble wash furniture. That's what it's or they are called, I'm not an antique expert, I don't know. But they would go to England for four months of the year, driving around antique hunting and shipping them to the cape without insurance.

The ship they were using had a flood, and if you don't know marble, it takes water spots/marks and can't come out with any kind of refurbishment. They lost all their money and sold the house to move to Detroit, Michigan where my brother, Alan, had a job for Lester that he interviewed for and got.

Alan starts his stupid ways after so many years and tells me: "Do you know, Susan, how I fixed them? I went to Europe for three years."

My parents had the time of their lives in Southfield, Michigan. They had a two-bedroom apartment and didn't care about Alan. Lester lost his job and then they moved back to the Boston area I forget where.

Alan was told by his boss, a general in the Army corps of engineers, "You don't have to go to Germany, Alan. You're a Jew."

Alan replied, "What a great way to see Europe."

He got twenty-five thousand dollars from Lester and some money of his own and bought a recreational vehicle with two bedrooms, one bath, etc. Braggart and a bore.

Military

Kill
or
be killed.

When it comes to the end, it's every man for himself.

```
                r         you
            a
         e
      h
   I
   Nigel                      Susan
                              I love you, Nigel,
                                    and all.
```

******

    I'm on the welfare for the welfare of the state and the welfare of the government—federal state and federal program. Direction of language (my brainstorming): let the motion carry. I love the people and I support you. Be very careful how you read. Keep your reading positive, forward. Government often sounds negative.

    The original calendar was not the lunar moon.

    You'll never be cold or hot or unfed or thirsty or not know the point of your own birth.

I've created a cover for your universal truth (Chomsky)—a greenhouse of sky. If you leave this earth, as America and Russia have, young ones, using math, I discovered language usage for travel.

Homeless for a month or so with the girls (we're kitties, we're kitties) I had the Laxinetas (Esther's brother's girl and family).

* * * * * *

Are you a paper tiger, Derek Miller?

Tiger! Tiger! burning bright
In the forest of the night,
What immortal hand or eye
Dare frame thy fearful symmetry?
—William Blake
(English literature sophomore year curriculum, Emerson College, Boston, Massachusetts.
Steph, in 2010, sold me a tiger bed rug for $5.00: huge, gorgeous.
All my writing is free thought.
No necessary order but what you may figure out beyond me.)
Jesus takes ministry; soothe my aching parts.
Nigel says to mommy, "Where's Derek?
Somewhere, a doctor is pulling Nigel's eyes backward, and Alan has a laser German gun, also a needle, that somewhere, he's putting it in and out of Nigel's eye.
Mommy, soothe, mommy, soothe doctors, including Kadoyan, Kasouki, and Miller. Take ministrations: "medication" to soothe my psyche?
Mommy has to go get Nigel. He's at #14 W (he didn't know) Grand Street.
Mommy's coming.
I saved your translucence; the very air you breathe was being contested. I existed as a general green color for you. I had no choice. Derek was opposed to free air. You were snug in your bed. Why it happened and I had to respond—?
Introducing Jesus.
What a thrill it would have been to us white kids to see black gospel singers come into the town of Milton, Massachusetts with necessary money to buy houses and open black churches for us all to hear the gospel of Motown: Detroit City. Starting at age eight, black music was on contemporary.

The use of the "N" word—nigger, nigger boy—is not an acquisition, it's a detriment to us all.

> Lester: "The niggers   Esther: She wants her niggers.
> are coming in three
> years."

Stop saying "shalom" to me. I'm not an Israeli (Jew). First, I went to a Jewish camp called Tevya in New Hampshire, for four years before they kicked me out. Esther and Lester had to come get me.

Stupid Alan was in the car. "It's not so bad being kicked out of camp, Susan," he said. Stupid Alan.

Then there came Camp Matoaka where I was voted the best captain of college competition (four teams).

Doin
the
Kina Hora

This was put up on the bulletin board at Holy Catholic Innocence Church here in Long Beach, California where I am residing now as I pull in my animals.

To all Parishioners

Two Jews rose from the knowledge of the Resurrection. Their names are/were Esther and Lester Shapiro.

The Head of the Church, Jesus Christ, from their beliefs had to deal with evil becoming associated with his name through the workings of the church.

The atrocities of the church are well-known to you through the insertions of "nice tight black asses."

Please advise your parish priests and the nuns who come here to worship—

Jesus is with me.

SBS (signed)
Susan Barbara Shapiro
This is a legal document, please do not remove.

When I came back, they had removed this document and left the thumb tacks neatly across the board.

✶✶✶✶✶✶

The only thing the Christians wouldn't forgive you for Christ was the Bay of Pigs. Catholic John Kennedy facing off with guerilla warfare's Fidel Castro and the hogs that had demons.

I've now given you a homework.

Two realities.

Do you know the sacrifice of Christmas?

The story of Esther by "who cares."

You're only as strong as your weakest link.

✶✶✶✶✶✶

Belief

Do you remember your "sight reading"? Don't move your lips when you read from left to right and back next line.

Then you learned "grammar" in grammar school.

A noun and a verb are necessary to be a sentence. Example, "Jesus wept."

Then you learned about adjectives, adverbs, demonstratives, and so on.

Then you learned about stress and unstressed sentences. These start the talking in your head. (Any language teachers are reading? I defer.)

Camp Tevya—I was an Israeli fighter since the age of eight. I was born in 1948, the same year Israel was formed as a nation. At Camp Matoaka, I was trained as an American warrior, just periods of baseball, volleyball, swimming, waterskiing, horseback riding, etc.

But at Tevya, I was brought up with Jewish pride. In Matoaka, I was raised through college competition, to have pride in America, Jewish style.

I didn't even know that "Susan" was an Arab name, meaning "princess of the Nile." When I went into Aaron Brothers frame shop, the merchant who helped me pick out frames for the pictures (Derek and Camilla the Nazi), Robert Darigol, was a monastery priest who came from a Jewish and Catholic parentage.

At fourteen, he went into the monastery (a gay boy - faggot) hunter green orange color colors from enlightenment

He got a doctorate in religion that he felt was nothing. He had a mental disorder called "manic depression." One of his first gay experiences was with Barry Manilow (not a good "lover") according to Robert. He writes about "highs and lows and anywhere I possibly can." Robert thinks it's mental. Remember people, a good mentality is what your teachers strive for. You've termed this the wrong way and psychiatry is following suit by medicating people who are harmless and usually advanced by your idea of mental illness. You've really failed yourselves by who you termed "mentally ill."

I've told you the story of Noah, and "hearing voices." It's very dangerous to allow this to carry as motion. Heed my words.

You can't shoot a man without taking responsibility for his life.

Wrong way, Mr. Bush, it's not a negative response. It's not life in prison. Never say die.

Hildy Gurney sent me a DVD called *My Favorite Thing* with Peter O'Toole. I saw it at Robert's house. It was the funniest movie I've ever seen.

She sent it unopened and old and said: "Thank you for my eye." It was sent by way of the computer and Robert's sister picked it up so Robert said it was his.

Let me explain: I learned how to create to bring up our boys who've died for their country and anybody who has been desecrated by we, the people. Hildy was the first to tell me that I have succeeded. It was an emotional time in my life, about three years ago. I've been working my life to the cause of restoring the people to youthfulness and good health, starting with good bones.

I was always concerned that I'd be late and there would be dead bones.

I've been sidetracked by the weak, evil, and boring God and his chosen people. They are against real advancement in man's higher state of being. If I'm the Lord, like Jesus, and I'm not his kind of Lord to Lord over you, I want you to have everything you'd ever dreamed of without even knowing I had anything to do with it. I might now be thwarting that effort. I just want to walk amongst you. Parents and God are my enemies. Sorry, for "we" who believed for so long in his good grace. He cuts throats, brings up the eye, and what's in between can't be seen. I hope I'm not too late for your sake and mine, too. I'm only human just like you.

My ultimate destination is Palm Desert. It is home to the domestic short hair: Nigel, the sire and Nigela, his child. He's neutered, how did it happen? Only the gods know. But it did. Angelica is Persian, they're fraternal twins. And Montrose, the Maltese, is head breed and he's the head of his breed. The Great Dane is next breed but it's been a long time since I've seen one.

Do you remember during World War II that the Nazis came to Denmark and the King put a Hebrew arm band on and then his people followed suit. Every person wore the Star of David's arm band and the King told the Nazis: we are all Jewish.

The Nazis left.

Snow White and Cinderella sat down one day to talk about love forever true.

* * * * * *

Song

Did you create something you can't manage, America? The becoming of a fascist state? Everybody was overseas fighting the fight of fights. At home? Esther and Lester were fascists. I grew up for twenty years under this man's house. It was very unpleasant, but the woman softened the time by graciousness toward me. She could control the fascist (gray, red, and white) vocally. "Come on, Lester."

At the Green Hotel and Apartments where Nigel and I lived together for ten years, I struggled with communicative disorders: studying it (lifetime it seems) and struggling with it around me. Truth and sense were achieved in my talking eyes. Where they came from? But I heard a voice that said:

Nigel has stimulating conversation. He will live forever, Egypt. My very dear loves, I'll never forget this.

Nigel and I are separated now by location. He escaped death in San Gabriel's pound when Andrew took us out through bringing the cops to our door. He told them I had no food and was dying. They took me to a behavioral center of Alhambra hospital where a young, good-looking doctor of psychiatry ruled out, finally, all and any mental illness associated with me. Nigel was left in Andrew's care to give him his insulin shots. Nobody can do it but me.

Now, I hear that the people he lives with are giving him pills. He can't take pills, that's why I was glad he needed shots. He closes his mouth and eyes and brings up his front paws and squeezes his mouth shut until he needs to breathe, and you shove the pill in. I know, I've tried myself. Where I failed (feeling sorry for him and afraid), they are succeeding. He's still alive. Thank you, but Mommy's still coming.

When "hearing voices" first started, I would look around and ask: who are you? Then as I became more interested in teaching, I would say: Stand up and say your name.

I saw outside my window of 570 E. Dayman Street, a lovely lady in black and white, sporting high heels.

She looks, in her white jacket and matching skirt, a lady coming home from church. She crossed the street, diagonal to me as if she now starts her ministry.

My lovely boss, Tenyka Sheriff, is sometimes religious—I've seen her lose it and bring up the bone of Christ.

For Christmas last year, I sent her *The Bread of Life* and *Today in the Word*. They're prayer verses that you start out your daily life. I found them to be soothing even when not needed.

People
love
me.

A life force, and I like this life in its difference of being different to any I've ever known. It keeps privacy in God's world where Nigel and I live to my life's forces of work for your sake. It's doable.

The prophesy of Lord Jesus Christ is self-needed.

Chekov from Star Trek: Europe? We Russians invented it.

* * * * * *

Is the hard life winning over the good life, America?
Race, culture, and creed: belief—my credo
I get it. Thank you, America.

* * * * * *

Alan Shapiro, first true traitor since Benedict(ine?).
Arnold

* * * * * *

Language usage

"Voices": audiological recognition of a physical fact.
I'm trying to get the communicative process here into this field of psychiatry from ASHA (American Speech and Hearing Association) national. It's criminal not to take an active part in the mental concept of "are you hearing voices?"
How is your state of mind, America? Can you hold?

* * * * * *

To Nancy Miller, Derek's stepmom and advisor and the wife of Joel Miller (my first husband till he finished his army reserves training. That's seven years, and Derek was born. When Derek turned two, we were gone from our Joel's house where he was born in Lexington, Massachusetts), Nancy who, under the cover of Joel, put up $100,000 per year for Derek's bachelor's degree from Sarah Lawrence. If I succeed here, I will send across the States a purple rose and $100,000 naturally from California to Boston beginning in Tennessee with Elvis Presley's "Bridge over Troubled Waters." From Richard Sheehan and Susan Shapiro, and the family of dog and cats.
With love, to Nancy Miller
SBS

* * * * * *

Hope I make it.

I'm a majority of one.

Mental illness doesn't exist. It's all in your head.

* * * * * *

I'm working on Jesus Christ's "eternal life" concept using the practical application process.

I leave you, my dear reader, without any knowledge of how I go about much of what I give you as statements of facts, quotables, and small stories.

It's a teaching method where you try to figure out how and what I mean. That way, dear reader, I have you, too, working on these subjects and quotables, and hence, alternate realities would come.

You have the job.

Back to work.

Don't ever deny yourself opportunity.

* * * * * *

Have you known for years that Christ's church offended small sex children?

Register them under you as such. It's beyond necessary today. Orange Faggots and hunter green gay pride are here. And I have been around them orange hunter green for fourteen years. I love them. But I know the predator in them, and I've spent much time watching over children. Adults? Them, too.

When in truth, white structure comes in and Cheryl Laxineta Goldachich DDS with her wet tongue, her inoperable articulators, her mental attitude, and her disgusting sex desire, boyish manners, big bullabusta (evil level of brown belt in karate). God slits your throats, America. And the vision I see is general acceptance of her ill behavior.

It's disgusting. Stop it.

* * * * * *

I'm still a speech hearing and language teacher, uncredentialed because I go on my own way. And the sensory approach I take of observable verbal behavior is way superior to psychology: three modalities to verbal communication—aggressive, assertive, and passive. I qualify my speech as assertive behavior (word usage).

I called my friend Janie in Brookline, Massachusetts where John F. Kennedy was born. His house is green (hunter green). I asked her if I were an assertive personality. She responded: "No one is more passive than you."

* * * * * *

My significant other
Sociology Tuesday Thursday
1966, C.W. Post Brookville New York.

Sex is just an act. Real sex begins and culminates in love. Sex is impossible for most girls. I would like to hope it's also the same for boys. It depends on the partner's finesse. Finesse comes in the discovery of each other when love is true.

* * * * * *

Country 105 FM

They called 'em crazy (rust and burnt green) when they started out. Said seventeen's too young to know what love's about. They've been together for fifty-eight years now, ain't that crazy?

* * * * * *

Everything you do comes back to you.
Protect your own ass.
You will know Christ for what you have done to yourself as man.
Do you know that "the beat of the day" takes place when the complete enjoyment of the pain in another being begins?

* * * * * *

Alan Shapiro
Barrington, R.I. (Mine and Richard's house using his salary and the hold of Lester's puny money.)
"One person should be in total pain so I can feel more like a man"
Derek present, physiological reaction, and then Alan...

Oh

My

God,

is missing.

* * * * * *

The 20,000 index cards of mine are in a burgundy carry-on vinyl airline bag.

* * * * * *

When I had to leave everything behind to take care of Nigel's twins, I made it home February 26th, Nigel didn't.

* * * * * *

Don't take a hand out, put a hand in.

* * * * * *

I've been at Hitler's youth camp a long time ago.

When the Jews were entrapped, they complained about the starvation. Hitler said (as Susan or in my mind how I'd react), "Just think how skinny you'll be."

I ran the whole way.

Everybody has always said, "Susan's getting skinny, what's wrong with Susan?

I've been skinny since Esther called me "fat" at fifteen or sixteen years old. I don't know how much I weighed, but I danced in my room or down the basement four hours without stopping. When I'd get hungry, I'd dance another hour. I knew how to throw up (Ellen Euse taught me—thank you; no need anymore).

I've weighed in at eighty-one pounds since Glendale Adventist (me?) Medical Center, with Ara Kadoyan in the lead.

I now weigh about ninety-two pounds, the most I've weighed in twenty years. Eating everything I love and no weight gain. I know how to eat. Right up to three good bites and that's it. And you'll live eternal life.

Now, I'm a mental athlete, and the weight gain is slow yet steady so I am still okay. I'm very particular how I look and now, instead of an

extra small in the junior department, I'm became a small. It's time now to try to cut back. I'm in a new environment and my eating habits are different. Quality of food is lacking.

D

Derek Miller worked many years for the United Nations, specializing in research of African affairs with a partner and a boss, a geology expert.

He gave many presentations. How has his affect/effect been on this world? Here I am and, wow, the pain I'm suffering. Is my nation suffering as poorly as I am bodily? (My genitals have been charged, still celibate but without my Nigel.)

Derek, according to Lester (Dead Lester), wrote essays for the graduate record exams. Went to Oxford University (wasn't happy), but graduated in Georgetown University, starting the *National Security Journal* for them as founding "editor."

Now, he's a father and a teacher, and like me at that age, a private tutor. His Nazi wife works, and they live in Norway together where Derek is coming out of a five-year project to give a lecture to NATO.

Little Derek

Old joke

What's a Jewish wife's favorite whine? Wine?
"I want to go to Miami."

* * * * * *

The Enemy's from Within.

In Lexington, Massachusetts, I turned twenty-one on my honeymoon with Joel (that's another story). I registered to vote. I raised my

hand and touched the Bible and was asked, "Will you protect your country from enemies from both within or without?" Continued and rewritten on next page.

I swore on a Bible in Lexington, Massachusetts, as I registered to vote (twenty-one years old).

"Do you swear to protect your country from enemies both from foreign or domestic?"

I swore: "Yes, I do."

He said, "Congratulations, you may now vote. Election day is on the second of November every general election. I got my newsprint bulletin with all the propositions and electorate hopefuls. I've answered for or against all the proposals and you are allowed to take this in to the voting booth. I'm a registered Republican. I went for the one who pulled in the belt and ran back for his buddy."

* * * * * *

Here I come, Nigel, Montrose the Maltese, Nigela, and Angelica as fast as I can.

On February 26th, Nigel and I were separated as you know. Montrose, Nigela, and Angelica were adopted out. I couldn't get there fast enough. Cheryl Goldasich was still and still is coming at me, getting in front. And our pain is extreme.

Back off Cheryl. She's a boy, bobs her head when she speaks, has a wet and awful tongue, which I will not acknowledge, recognize, or realize for your sake.

At first, there was
God and a tree.

Then there was Esther

Then there was

Your mother is a sicko,

A book that is missing

God
is a
sicko.
I've got it back.

Maybe people of great religious belief and faith will hear these words and laugh a moment out of seriousness to realize that God's problems are possibly worse than yours.

Mental house admittance: work your own problems out.
I laughed, too,
Me, (and God?),

Esther to Derek (my son).

I always tell Derek, "Your mother's a sicko but she loves you."
This she's telling me in her home.
In my house, she isn't allowed to say a word. I'd kill her, but she'd let's go her eyes and wouldn't feel a thing. So, it's not worth death or prison to kill either one.
I left it, during my life, that the two, are assholes, who'd listen?
Then they got desperate (over what, I've never known) and found a lawyer who isn't a lawyer. Part of their alliance for the mentally ill (them).
I've never involved myself with their beliefs. I have reached a point in my life where I took the doctor's pill. I did "hear voices." They just start talking right through me. But I've never told anyone I knew— either Esther or Lester—that this was part of my existence, and that I worked against it by creating areas that they could improve from negative stimuli to positive stimuli and my responses were understandable.

I got stopped
between a rock and a hard space.
I'm still here. The only speech hearing
therapist/scientist involved.

Communicative disorders department of the California State University is going to get involved because I'm going to shame them into it.
105 FM.
God is great,
beer is good,
and people are crazy.

The next book is called:

A Return to Yesteryear,

        a Hearty

                Heigh-Ho Silver

                  Away

How am I doing so far?

The End
So it begins,
I Believe.

www.ingramcontent.com/pod-product-compliance
Lightning Source LLC
Chambersburg PA
CBHW060638290526
45793CB00001B/308